PURPOSE FROM ADVERSITY

THE BIOGRAPHY OF EUNAN C. ANYAIBE

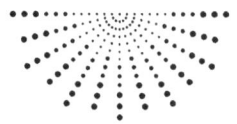

EUNAN C. ANYAIBE
NANDI CHARLES

SELF PUBLISHED

All rights reserved. No part of this book may be reproduced or transmitted in any form or by any means without written permission from the author.

Copyright © 2024 by Eunan C. Anyaibe and Nandi Charles. All rights reserved.

No portion of this book may be reproduced in any form without written permission from the publisher or author, except as permitted by U.S. copyright law.

Book Cover Design by ebooklaunch.com.

ISBN: 979-8-9898204-2-9

❦ Created with Vellum

I dedicate this book to my parents Suzanne and Kelvin Anyaibe. I also dedicate it to the love of my life, Nandi Charles and our kids. It was written from a place where my heart is at peace and that is the village of Umueleagwa [Onicha, Ezinihitte Mbaise], Imo State in Nigeria. I am a son of that land and irrespective of how many things I have amassed in this life, I will never be able to forget my humble beginnings. I am a devoted Igbo individual, deeply rooted in the rich traditions and values that I would never deviate from, and that I hold close to my heart. This book is dedicated to all the people back home and to all current readers who have found something to resonate with as they read this book.

Thank you,
EA.

FOREWORD

A month after meeting Chike through a chance encounter, I knew there was something very different about him. He was not like every other man I had ever spoken to. It was almost like talking to a male version of myself. I knew right then that we would have a long, fruitful future together. He is one of the most confident people I have ever met. He knows exactly what he wants out of life and has so many ideas that are much bigger than himself. This book will serve as a guide to others who may be experiencing the same trials, tribulations, frustrations, and who need a sliver of hope of succeeding in life after adversity. He is a wonderful father and partner, both personally and professionally, and he has a generous spirit that keeps on giving, even to a fault. I hope that this book, conceived by him but written by me, finds a place in your heart and your bookshelf.

Sincerely,
    NC

PREFACE

I have always had a burning desire to put the pen to paper and paint a canvas of what is in my heart for the world to see. It has always been my passion to reach others on a platform where I can share experiences to foster much needed healing and healthy dialogue. I struggled with many obstacles along the way, some of which left indelible memories and experiences that I am now very comfortable sharing. My hope is that these stories, which are all part of my journey in this life, will motivate and inspire others to know that they are not alone and that there is life, hope and the ability to find purpose after adversity.

My future wife and best friend, Nandi Charles, has played a tremendous role in helping me to put together this book. Together, we have great ideas that seem to come together seamlessly. As my soul mate and twin flame, we work in partnership with everything we do, from our personal lives to our professional ones, she is my life partner.

Lastly, it is my hope that the people of Mbaise will appreciate the language used and the context of this text as it paints a story introducing a son of their land to the world stage. My story puts a face to one of the countless souls from this region and is a cautionary tale of how easily situations can go downhill if measures are not taken to remedy them.

TABLE OF CONTENTS

Introduction

Chapter 1
West African Woes and the Western Power
Nigeria & The Biafra Perspective
Chapter 2
Born in Abia but raised in Umueleagwa & Owerri
Ancestral Ties to Umueleagwa & Family Upbringing
Chapter 3
Caught up: A Habitual Life of Partying and Numbness to Love
Chapter 4
Health Struggles and A Call to Duty Within My Family
Chapter 5
Hope for A Better Tomorrow: Migration to India
Chapter 6
Obstacles and Struggles: Finding My Way to Financial Security
Chapter 7
Investing in Love: Heartbroken With Sorrow
Chapter 8
How Hitting Rock Bottom Transformed My Spiritual Life

Chapter 9
Immigration Barriers: Surviving My Fears and Struggles
Chapter 10
A Chance Encounter Leads To A Forever Partnership in Love
Chapter 11
A Return to Umueleagwa And Finding My True Purpose In Life
Chapter 12
A Critical Analysis of How Failures Shortchange Our Youths
Chapter 13
Seeking My Destiny One Plan At A Time
Chapter 14
Strategies For Success After Failures and Disappointments in Life [87]
About the Authors

INTRODUCTION

This book serves to showcase the beauty of Igboland traditions and West Africa in general. It also highlights the traumas of the continent at the hands of the Western world's need for resources. There is a focus on how these dynamics affect socio-economic structures, family values and cultural norms. In this text, we will explore both on a community level, how these forces negatively affect the stability of citizens in this region, and how it impacted my own journey, which is not an uncommon one.

I am placing myself at the forefront of this discussion and giving readers a glimpse into the realities that exist in African communities, the struggles and the unsavory decisions that sometimes must be made to get by. I want the plight of these people to be seen on an international platform so that dialogue for change can be sown and one day reaped to benefit the continent.

My passion lies in being a tool of change that is instrumental in the development of my community and people. I have always

INTRODUCTION

been a man of culture, and especially proud of being an Igbo man because it is one of the things that defines me. Though others may not understand that connection, but without that meaningful attachment, I would not be the man that I am today. Identity is important in the journey of 1000 men, it has always shaped civilizations and will continue to be the thing from which we pull from to build our future tomorrow.

1
WEST AFRICAN WOES AND THE WESTERN POWERS

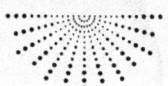

*L*ike white on rice, the West has always had its interests in the continent of Africa. One of the richest prime real estate locations on the globe, the continent of Africa extends a treasure trove of natural resources. But who could blame them when Africa has always been the breadbasket of the world, creating some of the world's firsthand axes and fire manipulation techniques.

Africa has become a supply powerhouse with 40% of its gold being exported and 90% of its chromium and platinum being taken by nations outside of the continent. It has the largest reserves for cobalt, diamonds, uranium, and gas. The world's insatiable appetite for Starbucks coffee, newest name brand cell phones to the latest cars, all push the pressure for western nations to tap into these resources beyond their shores and into the backyard of African nations.

Have a need for a sweet tooth? Next time you chomp down on that candy bar be sure to think of Africa because, thanks to Ghana and the Ivory Coast which provides 70% of the world's cocoa, such a delicious creation is possible.

Let's look at the marine fishery industry on the continent.

West Africa exports 4.5 million tons of fish overseas while places like Namibia and South Africa are exporting 80% to 90% of their fishes annually.

Think this trend only extends to food exports and natural resources? Not at all, it also indirectly affects other types of industries like the aerospace and military industries. These sectors use that cobalt to create superalloys that are used in jet engines and fighter jet aircraft models. Other areas of use include the manufacturing of automobile airbags, drying agents found in paints, varnishes, and inks which are found in pens.

Our resources are being used to create dyes for clothing and food industries that supply mass global cuisines and food products for "developed countries". Our natural resources are being used to create gas turbines, high speed steels, conversion of synthetic fuels from natural gases and removal of sulfur moieties from petroleum and natural gases. Carbon steels are also exported in large quantities to be used for construction bars, beams, coils, sheets, rods, and fasteners.

So far, we have only taken a peep at natural resources exploitation. We haven't even looked at the inventions courtesy of Africa to the rest of the world. For starters, upon examining the Lebombo bone found in the Lebombo Mountains of Swaziland, that dates to 35,000 B.C, we can easily see that Africa has blessed the world with one of the oldest mathematical inventions. Use of several medical procedures like vaccinations, autopsy procedures, dental operations, skin grafting, anesthesia, caesarean sections date back to 2750 B.C in Africa; notably in regions like Egypt, Uganda and Rwanda.

This mere scratch on the surface just unravels some of the very important contributions Africa has made to the West. If we examine the indirect contributions Africa has made to the Western nations, we can think about the Transatlantic Slave Trade. This horrific event was responsible for bringing to the West many enslaved Africans to the Americas. This impacted life in the Caribbean, South America, Central America, North America and even Europe. This singular act contributed to new and different techniques in cooking, fashion and style, diversity in musical genres, cuisines, linguistic dialects and financial prosperity to industries and economies.

* * *

AFTER THOUGHTS

What is the result of all these exports of our natural resources? Poverty levels in these regions are still at an all-time high, which creates an almost non-existent middle class. People are either very wealthy or in abject financial strains. If we are supplying so much to the world, why are those gains not seen in a tangible way in our communities and standard of living?

EFFECTS OF THE GROSS OVER HARVEST

Over-harvesting of resources is destroying livelihoods in Africa. It is leading to extinctions, loss of biodiversity, damage to the ecosystem and crops, which affects communities widespread. Let us review the situation in the Niger Delta region of Nigeria. Many foreign companies that come to this region make no win contractual agreements with the Nigerian government, which never benefit the citizens of Nigeria or the locals of Niger Delta. It just makes financial gains for a few government officials and the foreign companies that come to extract and retrieve. Another more pressing conundrum with this set up is that these expatriate companies bring in their own workforce from overseas and neglect to hire local Nigerian citizens who are equally qualified.

This is why we often observe graduates transitioning to

careers outside the scope of their studies; a chemical engineer becoming a bank manager or a doctor turning into a politician.

Too often, young people are disillusioned with the bleak future job prospects knowing fully well that after graduation, they will not be given a job on their own merits, but rather will be overlooked by nepotism and tribalism based on a system that rewards who you know rather than what you are qualified to do.

Professionals in education, finance and accounting are waiting six to eight months for a paycheck after working tirelessly each day to meet the demands of their jobs. How can pensioners who paid into a system for many years be told they would have an eight month wait just to receive funds to maintain themselves? The mismanagement of funds and contract money makes for a job force that is grossly underpaid and undervalued. No wonder Nigeria and other West African nations are experiencing massive brain drain. Days without electricity, public health issues with malaria, potholed roads that are built with cheap materials by irresponsible foreign companies all tell the story of why there is a brain flight out of the country once folks have an opportunity for greener pastures.

* * *

Nigerians are hoping and praying for a better time to come, a better day ahead and a better situation for themselves and their families. These plights lead to desperation in the eyes of those younger people who seek stability and financial mobility. One wonders why a university graduate may trade in their education for a seat in the driver's seat of scamming and online fraud. They see a steady flow of income and soon their education becomes useless.

The Nigerian government has an obligation to do better for

its citizens because we believe so much in our institutions. We stand by them as a people, and we are proud of our identity.

But what is there to be proud of when we are treated less than, when we are treated as second class citizens by a system that only cares about its wealth stakeholders and its own self interests.

We are never made a priority when these secret deals and contracts are negotiated between our government and these foreign western countries. Why won't the government put its citizens first and work on developing us as a people, a community and as a nation?

To build a better nation, we must invest in our own and we should lift our people through programs that help them to realize their untapped abilities and reach their highest potential in life.

This is a small price to pay toward paying it forward on the ideals that our future generations are the ones that will become our future professionals and work force. We must start caring about our citizens and catering toward their progress because once we take care of them, they will take care of our nation.

* * *

Nigeria & The Biafra Perspective

Seven years after Nigeria's independence from Britain, the Nigerian Civil War commenced. This war, known as the Biafra War, was caused by several different factors that negatively impacted the Igbo community. These included not being respected as an ethnic group, having lack of access to economic advancements and the control of religious and oil resources in Igboland.

Igbo people were frustrated with discriminatory practices in politics, economics and social settings which stagnated their social mobility and political aspirations in the Nigerian society.

Feeling disillusioned and isolated, Igbo people began to voice their desires to secede from the rest of Nigeria to unify as a people and find greener pastures as a community.

Instead of being able to peacefully exist and form their own entity as a people, they were instead cornered by other ethnic groups and the Nigerian government. The main way of transport into the Igbo community, which at the time was the Niger Bridge, was blown up and this created problems for food to the masses.

In the aftermath of things, more than half a million civilians were killed and around 100,000 military Biafra soldiers were casualties. The atrocity count was so high that the civil war quickly made international headlines and was shown on the television screens for all to see in the West.

PROSPECTS FOR THE FUTURE AS A BIAFRA

Today many descendants of the Biafra still believe that they face discriminatory practices in the Nigerian society. They feel that they are passed over for contracts and not given a fighting chance as a fellow Nigerian to tap into resources. There is a feeling that we are not seen as competent to be rulers in Nigeria politically. Igbos have made significant contributions to the Nigerian landscape in technology, business enterprise to industry productions. Many Igbos in the diaspora are also making great strides in entertainment, sports, the food industry, business, public service, and education.

In parts of Nigeria, in the north and in the Lagos area, there are many accounts of Igbo people being killed due to discriminatory practices that are anti-Igbo. Many Igbos are being run out of their businesses due to instability and threats on their lives due to tribalism and irritation with the growth success rates.

As a child growing up in Nigeria, I enjoyed the stories my dad would tell me about his time in the Biafra war as a signal officer. His position was a very important role that helped with transmission of intel and data between the ranks. He would tell us about his memories of working in the command center and controlling the communication and messaging systems.

2
BORN IN ABIA BUT RAISED IN UMUELEAGWA AND OWERRI

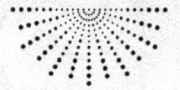

Born in Abia but Raised in Umueleagwa and Owerri

I was born Eunan Chikezie Anyaibe on April 4th, 1984, to Suzanne and Kelvin Anyaibe in a city called Aba located in Abia State, Nigeria.

I HAVE LIVED IN QUITE A FEW PLACES

Born into a family of seven siblings and two working class parents, I was the last child. At around the tender age of seven years old, my parents packed up and moved us to Owerri in search of greener pastures. Around this time, my parents were trying to start up a restaurant business and so they sent me along with several of my siblings into the village to stay with relatives whilst they worked on getting the family business to blossom.

In our household, it was all hands-on deck. Everyone helped in any way they could, from helping to sell food on the street to taking on chores and tasks delegated. Per my grandmother's daily instruction, I was expected to pick firewood for cooking and fetch water for domestic purposes. She would also have me harvest provisions and items from her family farm. My grandmother knew how to conserve the little she had. She would often stretch out many of the soups and foods she prepared so that we had food to eat. She taught me the art of conservation and resource management. During my time with her we ate mostly fish and fresh vegetables because she could not eat meats with hard textures. She would send me out to hunt for snails, climb trees to get fruits and gather ingredients for cooking. At an early age I learned the principle of fending for myself. Little did my grandmother realize that she was teaching me the value of being resourceful and dedicated to completing tasks. To some, it may appear as a struggle but to me, these hardships have helped me to build character and perseverance.

* * *

Being in the village of Umueleagwa has had a profound impact on my perspective as an Igbo man. During this time frame, I had become more culturally aware of my identity as a son of the land and more appreciative of what being from Mbaise means.

Out of all my siblings, I am the only one who has had the strongest connections both culturally and spiritually to our ancestral village of Umueleagwa. The time spent with my grandmother created a great impact on my value system and adherence of Igbo cultures and traditions.

What does it mean to be an Igbo man from Umueleagwa? It means having a moral compass that promotes fairness, knowing your culture very well and standing on the side of truth and common decency.

In our village, children are taught to respect their elders and respect the chain of command in the home between gender roles. When your parents are getting up in age, it is the responsibility of their children to nurture, protect and care for them.

Igbo traditional expectations dictate that most childbearing men be married by the age of 30 and to start a family of their own. This unspoken rule pushes the ideals that Igbo men will begin to establish their position in the role of being a man sooner than later. He is supposed to own land, establish his home, and take care of his own family. A measure of great achievement to the Igbo family is the reliance on their children taking on a role as provider. The more their offspring can provide financial stability for the family, the more they feel a strong sense of pride and fulfillment. This extends to the idea that taking care of your parents will equate to having a life that is smooth sailing and filled with good karma. Other major focus points in our culture include women giving birth to babies. This is seen as a blessing for family lineage continuation in Igbo tradition. Our name and longevity are tremendously significant to our culture, that having children is attached with burial rites, a practice deeply ingrained in Igbo culture. In our community, when parents pass away or meet with their ancestors, the children are supposed to perform burial rites and give their parents a good farewell celebration. This is why we value the practice of taking our kids back to our villages and keeping them cultured in our traditions, so that they may not depart from our ways and teachings. This unspoken obligation is especially expected to carry on with male children to their fathers. It is no wonder that most of our Igbo traditions and practices are very much patriarchal in nature.

Our culture also has a strong belief in reincarnation. We believe that when you do good in your past life, that same energy will follow you into another life and if you do unsavory things, the same karma will follow you into the afterlife.

Our culture forbids our children to engage in activities that are shameful to the family name. If revealed, such a person can be banished or disowned by the family members because their behaviors and moral compass are not in alignment with our traditions and expectations in Igboland.

* * *

Ancestral Ties to Umueleagwa & Family Upbringings

My dad, Kelvin Anyaibe is from the village of Umueleagwa. How the story goes is, my dad comes from a family of seven, four sisters and two brothers. He was raised in a Catholic family and started working from a very young age in the home of Chief Sir Festus Okeahialam. Here he would help with chores and complete day-to-day activities while attending school to help support his family. My dad was such a hard-working man who was very dedicated to reaching his goals in life. He really left an indelible mark on a young budding Chike. He was such an enterprising and self-sufficient man, I admired his work ethic and often strived to emulate it. He was one of the motivating forces that inspired me to also have a hustling spirit and good business acumen.

My mother, Suzanne Anyaibe, is from the village of Omukwu and is also from a Catholic family consisting of seven siblings. She began her journey from a young age working in the market and helping relatives with sales of food products. Little did my mother know, this is where she would eventually meet my dad and their love story would commence. She would go on to be a great mother and a committed wife to my dad. They worked tirelessly together to take care of us. When I remember my mother, I see her as someone who was able to manage multiple things simultaneously, from auditing the finances to making time for her children and ensuring that the house was filled with food and love. She was indeed a great role model to me and my siblings. She showed us what being strong and compassionate was all about.

My parents' story is one of strength, devotion, and commitment to each other. I have never seen a couple more dedicated and in love than my parents. Even when they have arguments, they can quickly reconcile and work things out. This is evidenced by them teaming up against outside forces that intervene in their relationship matters. After 53 years of marriage, they are no longer just lovers but are now forever companions and best friends. I too aspire to have such a long extended marital journey with my future wife.

Our parents instilled the values of having a good work ethic, being industrious, having family values and showing generosity. They have taught us the moral duty to serve your community and what a healthy marriage with longevity should look like. They have shown us how to try repeatedly when we encounter mistakes and how to be loyal to those who helped us along the way.

3
CAUGHT UP: A HABITUAL LIFE OF PARTYING AND NUMBNESS TO LOVE

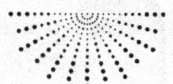

It was 2005, I was just getting into my grove as a college freshman studying civil engineering, when I was told that I would have to stop my education to allow my siblings to finish their own. While this was disappointing, we were raised to help family members. Putting my own dreams aside, I tried my hands at real estate and began work as an agent. During this time, I also went back to obtain a certificate in Culinary Arts to help widen my options in the job market.

Although I didn't get hired as a chef, I was able to work at my family's restaurant and prepare many of the cuisines I was trained to make from my schooling. During this time, my stress level was very high, so I relied on friends for comfort and emotional support. We were frisky and full of ourselves, roaming around town as young men like the world was ours. Soon I was trekking from one bar to the next pub drinking excessive amounts of alcohol with my buddies.

Did I care about my future at the time? Not really but I was doing what made me happy, and that was to have fun and enjoy my youthfulness. I went through a string of flings and love escapades where relationships lasted only a mere two weeks to six months. I remember all too well one relationship where I purchased my then girlfriend a cell phone. In less than two months, she was already in another man's arms. It was such a painful experience for me as a young man who had given his heart away only to be betrayed by someone I held in high regard. But such is life and what I know now as a man that I did not as a youth, is that with each experience, there is room to learn and grow.

I did many careless things in my short-term relationships with women. Making promises to them I had no intention of keeping, playing the game of lust and pulling out from them emotionally before they could even wink their eyes. I did some things that I am ashamed of, and it was because I was not mature and acting like an adult at the time. The things of yesterday are old and childish, and the mindset of today is one whereby I value people, respect them, and cherish them for the invaluable traits they bring to the table.

In my short-term relationships, I never allowed myself to enter into and have meaningful connections with my suitors. I was so unsure about whether I would ever settle down or ever marry. I did not trust women enough to feel comfortable with prioritizing their emotions or feelings. All I could think about was myself and my own emotions and selfishly indulge myself. Today, I can honestly say that I do apologize to all and any woman out there that I may have done wrong to in the past. If I could give you a hug today, I certainly would and if I could say something to you, I would say that I am sorry, and you are worthy of true happiness and love.

The boy I was at 23 years old is not a mirror reflection of the man I have become at 39 years of age. I am a very different man, one who has changed and learned to love, compromise, appreciate and become compassionate and forgiving. My partner has brought out so many positive emotions in me, some I never even knew I had or would experience, all the while helping me to become a polished version of myself. I know that many of my childhood friends would find it unbelievable that a man like me would ever speak of love, much less talk of being in love. Surprisingly, these are the lyrics to my song and the pages of my story, one of redemption to cascades of love. I see the beauty in being in love with a soulmate and I value the benefits of finding it with the right person because that is one of the toughest things to find and hold onto.

4
HEALTH STRUGGLES AND A CALL TO DUTY WITHIN MY FAMILY

Years of standing on her feet and working in the industry of catering, my dear mother became very frail due to spinal conditions that deteriorated with time. I spent the next few years taking her for assessments and checkups at an orthopedic hospital in Enugu. One day as my mother was traveling on a bus, she experienced a medical emergency but was instead harassed by a fellow passenger who had neither the patience nor compassion towards her during her ordeal. Thanks to the graces of a few good-hearted Samaritans, she was able to get the immediate assistance she needed.

At this point, my siblings and I put our heads together and decided that it was best for her to schedule an operation to fix her spinal condition because it affected her urinary system. As we did our reviews of the hospitals in our neighborhood, we found that many of the patients who had similar surgeries had grave complications post-surgery. Some were even unable to walk until one full year later. With these dismal odds stacked against her, my oldest brother decided that it was best to fly our mother overseas for surgery in another country.

This was when we began to look at India as a destination to

take our mother for her operation. My eldest brother, who was a pharmacist, reached out to his contacts over there and began to book consultations with physicians and surgeons. We raised around 20,000 dollars and made the necessary arrangements and accommodations to ensure that she was flown out and treated to the best service that money could buy. Afraid of the unknown outcomes for my mother, I had to be strong for her because I was her son and she looked to me for strength.

We soon found ourselves booking flights to India and making accommodations for an extended stay. As my mother's surgery time approached, I was the only one out of my siblings to accompany her on the trip. I tended to her day and night like a husband would a wife, like a mother would have a child, like a lioness would her cub. Every day I combed her hair, gave her sweet baths, groomed her, and carried her in my arms. How quickly can the tables turn and yet time flies? Just yesterday she was carrying me as a baby and now it was my turn to carry her as my mom. She could rely on me to do everything for her, she could rely on me for emotional support and, more importantly, she could seek me out for comfort.

As we touched down in India, we were greeted by the staff of the Sparsh Hospital in Bangalore India. They were very hospitable and gave us a fine welcome to our hotel. From there, we spent another four days doing pre-operative testing and assessments. I was there with my mom, step by step, leading her every inch of the way and being her caregiver. During this time our unbreakable bond strengthened. Following the series of testing, Mom was rolled into the operating room theatre and surgery commenced. Back home, all eyes were clasped, fists tightened and minds on praying as we hoped for a successful surgery and a safe recovery. As we waited for word of her outcome, things began to take a strange turn when we noticed that she was not brought into recovery. Instead, my mother was placed in another area, sort of like an intensive care unit, to be observed. She looked like she was in a deep state of sleep, which we later found out was her body being in a comatose state, a complication of her surgery. One of the junior doctors then walked me downstairs to a bar that was near the hospital and asked me if I would like a stiff drink. We sat down and talked, and he let me know that he was not sure my mother would make it. He told me to prepare for the worst-case scenario as there was a possibility she would transition. It was devastating news for the entire family, and I was especially heartbroken because of the bond I shared with my mother. My sadness soon turned to anger as I pondered whether the doctors had done enough to save my mother's life. Was this trip even worth it? The cries of my dad and the wailing of my siblings on the phone pushed my mind into overdrive.

   I turned to the only place I knew how to when my back was against the wall and that was my Creator. I grabbed my mother's rosary and began my powerful prayers which lasted well into two hours. Two and a half hours into my prayers, I heard a voice say the words Uzenma and when I looked over, I saw that it came from my mother's lips. She had awakened from her comatose state and was calling out my older brother's name. Medical staff then moved her to recovery where she went in and out of consciousness. Again, we were told that she was experiencing complications from the procedure and was transported to another hospital facility that specialized in cardiology. They did several lab works and tests to screen her liver, heart, and other organs, trying to figure out how to stabilize her condition. At this time, I was frightened and afraid of the outcome, so much so that I felt so vulnerable. I could not save my mother and who else could if these doctors were also perplexed? As my mother was being transported, she gained consciousness and was terrified about getting into the ambulance. It brought back memories of her back in Nigeria where our ambulances mostly transport the dead not people that are alive. It is the opposite in the West and in Asia. She began to chastise the staff out of frustration, but I did my best to comfort her throughout her ordeal, which I recognized was not an easy one. About a week later, she was returned to the hospital where she had more surgery and put back into the recovery section. The doctors recommended that she become more active and practice walking, so I assisted her with each leg, one in front of the other until she was able to walk on her own.

I took her hand, held her, and helped her to move around and walk about on her own. Things were so different in the country of India for us that it took us two good days to get adjusted to even eating in the country. Eventually we sought out African restaurants, where I ended up meeting a Nigerian restaurant owner named Cliff. He was married to an Indian woman, and they had kids of their own. Cliff was from Anambra state and soon I took a closer interest in him as he showed me the ropes. On our first visit with my mother, he made us bitter leaf soup and we talked as we ate about job opportunities for Nigerians in India. He told us that his restaurant was a place I could network and meet fellow Nigerians. Once we were discharged from the hospital, we were told by the hospital staff to return to our hotel but instead we visited Cliff, where we met his mother. He seemed like a nice man, a family man, an Igbo man and so I was very comfortable. Later I would realize how far from the truth that was. All folk ain't kin folk. He extended his home to us to stay for 2000 rupees a day and since it was cheaper than staying at the hotel and we were around our own, we took him up on his offer. Around this time, I met a woman I would eventually become romantically involved with, and her name was Diana. She was an Indian chef working at the hospital and while I lived at Cliff's home, she would visit me. She would care for my mother and our bond would develop so deep that I contemplated marrying her. Since

I was turned off by her mother's pursuit of money, our relationship soon ended.

As time elapsed, I began to network with the Nigerian community at Cliff's restaurant. They advised me to put my mom on a one-way ticket back to Nigeria and to stay behind to hustle and find success in India. When I told my elder brother what my plan was, he was upset and disgusted, he told me to return to Nigeria and forget about India. I told my siblings I would return to Nigeria but only on one condition, and that was, if they paid for my ticket to return to India. They agreed and so I returned to India with the promise and hope of making it big but little did I know that the people who were advising me were merely unsavory entities looking to take advantage of fresh meat. It was a dog-eat-dog world out there, cold and every man for himself. How quickly I would fall prey. I stayed for a few months and continued to care for my mom in Nigeria. I then made up my mind to return to India.

5
HOPE FOR A BETTER TOMORROW: MIGRATION TO INDIA

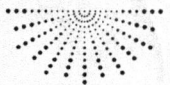

I returned to India and met with Cliff once again. This time I had around 3000 dollars on hand and a pocket full of dreams. He told me that he didn't want to be the one to introduce me to any illicit activities and so he would take me to a rural city in India to start a business with the money I had. For the next one to three years, I would buy and sell garments and engage in textile trading in the city of Tamil Nadu. The business was quite lucrative, so much so that I made around 100 dollars dividend a month which allowed me to acquire lands in Nigeria. However, after the third year in business, that venture became short-lived when the American dollar began to fluctuate in value. I wasn't making profits anymore and soon after I could not keep up with the fees to import my goods from the containers in India. This was when I made up my mind to leave Tamil Nadu and return to Bangalore. I gathered my belongings that were left in Cliff's house and made my way into my own place, a one-bedroom apartment. It wasn't upscale but it was just right for me at the time.

Jobless and without much to do, I began to gawk and wander around trying to find myself. I focused back on the

Nigerian community that frequented Cliff's restaurant. I began to wonder how they were able to live so well, driving fancy cars, living an upscale life, and flashing stacks of money. Quite the novice, but curious nevertheless, inquired and showed a vested interest in attaining that status too, but just what were they doing? I wanted to be just like them and so I pursued leads and nestled myself into social groups and networks. Eventually, I realized that many of these folks, if not an international student, an employed expatriate, or a legitimate business owner, were scamming or doing drug dealing.

With the little money that was left from the textile business that collapsed, it just wasn't enough to sustain my expenses and that led to me losing my apartment. I was broken inside and down on my luck, depressed, feeling alone and worst of all, homeless. To save face, I crashed at an associate's home who I knew very little about except that he was into the business of 419 [Scamming]. Who was I to judge him when I needed a place to stay and a safe space for me to get my head right? Meanwhile, I reflected on what my family back in Nigeria had told me. They made it known that they had prayed a special prayer that if I had ever done such things, I would perish and be doomed for life. That scared me straight from wanting to engage in risky and illicit affairs. The fear of a curse on one's head knows no shame like when your family won't even support you in bad deeds, and rightfully so.

I stayed with him nevertheless and he began to teach me the business he was doing. I observed how quickly he had victims in his clutches, and I realized how quick it was to make money doing this type of business. The next day I went to bed and had a dream in which I saw my mother telling me not to get involved in such things. It spooked me and I reached out to the guy and told him that I would not be able to get involved in his operations because I just didn't have a good feeling about it. I had strong inclinations that I would end up in trouble or, worse, shaming my family. Our family's name is so important to us, and we do not joke around when it comes to that. Irritated with my stance and blunt honesty, I was kicked out of his house and into the streets. Homeless once again, I returned to Cliff's restaurant to get advice on what other things I could do to put myself in a better situation.

As I entered the restaurant, people began to laugh and make fun of me. They saw me as a fool for turning down their unscrupulous business ventures. They called me a Mugu [Fool] and a simp, but my fear of my Creator, law enforcement and my family's namesake wouldn't let me continue down that path of no return. This is not the kind of life I want for myself. I come from an upstanding family and cheating people was not the right thing to do because I believe so much in karma. What energy you give out to the universe is what you get back in return.

Eventually, my sadness turned to alienation and the Nigerian community I had gotten so close to saw me as not enterprising solely because I refused to join in on the unscrupulous business activities that generated money illegally. I stayed steadfast to my Igbo traditions and customs and used them as my guiding force. I didn't have friends anymore and soon many folks disassociated from me because they felt I would snitch on them since I was not staying on code with their lifestyles.

When it rains, it truly pours. How truer an idiom could this one be than a reflection of my life? As I was at my lowest point, I met a man named George in that same Cliff's restaurant. You'd think by now I'd stop going to this place, but I was young and still learning my way in life. George was nicely dressed and immaculate in nature, gave the aura of exuding wealth and a man of means. He gave me a listening ear and, boy, did I pour my sorrows out on him. Not long after, he encouraged me to move into his flat with him. There I observed his business activities. Within a short space of time, I quickly figured out that he was doing two businesses: running scams and exporting drugs.

I had reached my breaking point and was tired of the environment I was in. There were no jobs for Nigerians here and I was not looking to marry anyone for papers. My opportunities were limited, and I was associating with people who were so desperate that they hustled in the wrong business ventures.

Within a week of staying with George, he advised me that he was traveling to Mumbai with his girlfriend and that I should stay in the house. She was a student and often cooked food for us in the apartment. The next day, I received a phone call from George ordering me to go to his room and remove a white stocking filled with some items under his bed. He asked me to take it to the restaurant and wait there as there were police officers getting ready to raid the apartments. By this time, my visa had expired, and the police would usually do raids to deport foreigners who overstayed their welcome. This created massive fear in me and, so thinking he was my friend, I grabbed the items without realizing what was happening. While on my way to the restaurant with the stocking and spotting the police check points, I accidentally ran into a Nigerian man on a bicycle, who I will call Jeff. I did not know this man, but I felt compelled to tell him my story. As the rose petals began to peel, I told him about George and what he ordered me to do. Jeff asked me to show him the items and, once inside, he showed me that it was cocaine. I was so dumbfounded because this was my first time ever seeing hard core narcotics. I could not believe how naïve I was and how easily I had been manipulated but what can I say, when you come from a family where you are brought up with decency, the streets can easily eat you up. My mind was blown, and I was afraid for my life. I began to think about what I had gotten myself into and how I could escape this. I quickly threw the bag of drugs to the side and ran pass the police check point.

Without thinking too much I quickly returned to Cliff's restaurant and was greeted by harsh words by fellow Nigerians who bashed me with insults for refusing to get my feet wet in the "lucrative" trade. They questioned why I had thrown away another person's drugs and not tried to use it to help myself out of poverty. In all my confusion, I was especially embarrassed by how quickly word had spread through the community about what was happening to me. They told me that I was in serious trouble because no deed goes undone. I told them that I can do any other business than scamming and drug peddling. This was when my eyes had opened about what these folks were getting into and what they were doing to upkeep their lavish lifestyles. I vowed to stay away from such business deals and to live my life on the righteous path. That same year, George gave me an ultimatum to pay him back for the drugs I had thrown away or I would not be around much longer. He and his street friends harassed me and made threats to my life. Feeling the pressure and fear, I quickly sold one of my lands in Nigeria for around 16,000 dollars and paid him back. This was to get him off my back while I figured out my future in India.

Now I was back to square one: no job, no place of my own, and not even a woman by my side. I started sleeping in the streets and was homeless once again. I lived like this for about six months. It was depressing and devastating, and I often wondered why the Creator made me this way, looking to stay righteous while suffering versus going the easy route in a life full of illicit deeds. Poverty was knocking at my door, but rather than do bad things to get money, I made the decision I would rather stay in poverty all in the name of keeping my dignity and family's namesake.

It got to the point where I was becoming ill and was unable to take care of myself. This was when I met Lincoln, another man who I had grown to know. He did not frequent the restaurant, but he knew some of the people I was faintly acquainted with. Lincoln was ordinary, very smart but he too fell prey to the streets chasing money and was involved in scamming. He said he noticed that I had a good heart and was not the type who could hurt others and still have a good night's sleep. Without rhyme or reason, he told me to go back into my business of selling clothing and offered for me to crash at his house until I could get back on my feet.

That was the beginning of a new start for me. I started doing trades in cotton and shirts made of cotton. This helped to sustain me until I was able to move into my own place once again. I know I have the gift of doing business and it's a blessing from the Creator to me. Every time I have bad times, I am always able to find a lucrative business to lift myself out of my predicaments and problematic situations.

6
OBSTACLES AND STRUGGLES: FINDING MY WAY TO FINANCIAL SECURITY

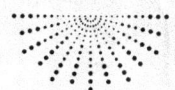

*I*t wasn't long before I began to feel the squeeze of not having all my ducks in a row. Time had passed and I wasn't getting any younger with little to no hope of achieving the type of financial freedom I desired. As I meditated, my mind was in a daze, trying to figure out how I could continue to support myself and send money back home to Nigeria to help my family out.

What seemed like an endless eternity of sorrow was quickly replaced with a glimmer of hope. It was something everyone else did to get by and by that, I meant almost every Nigerian who lived in India with an expired visa that was not a student. My duty to provide for my family back home and maintain myself made this lifestyle of doing underhand dealings look even more enticing as each day progressed. As I thought about my culture and traditions, I questioned my judgement. This was an act frowned upon in my culture but how do I take care of myself with no job, no papers, an expired visa and nowhere to turn. I had to survive even if it meant breaking ways with my traditions, breaking with my standards and convictions as a man of integrity. For integrity wouldn't help to put food on my table or pay my bills which were short term needs at the time.

So, there I was, throwing my hands in the bag of blackjack, playing a risky round of Russian roulette with life. Relying on my instincts to guide my way and take a walk down the path of success, I questioned the idea of taking the calculated risk despite the desperation. But wait! A voice said to me, "You are above this, do not even muddy the waters that come from within. Your Creator has a bigger purpose for your life. Stay strong my child for I have bigger dreams ahead for you."

I kept wondering if this voice was that of my deceased sister who was so close to me. I had been in India for so long, that I didn't even get to hold her close and tell her goodbye. That has always been something that I have deeply regretted, and it has haunted me for the longest time. Instead, I left it in the hands of my Creator and prayed day and night. I did whatever side hustle I could from working construction to selling hair, t-shirts and removing debris from demolition sites just to get by.

When I got my money, I would invite some homeless people to my apartment, cook food, and eat with them. Most might find this practice to be weirdly eccentric, but it gave me peace of mind. I too was once homeless, and I saw those people as my own. I saw my struggles and demons as their struggles and demons. I knew what they were going through, and I needed company in a place where I was left so alone and lonely. I believe so strongly in karma, that what good energy I give out there will come back to me tenfold.

As time progressed, these four people I had dinner and lunch with every day became like family. We would laugh together, be sad together and talk about the latest things happening in the Nigerian community. I remember fondly watching the Cable News Network in America because that is where I got most of my news. It felt like home away from home even with them being drunkards and aimless souls.

One evening, one of the men we ate with named Junior knocked at the door. About an hour earlier, we received a phone call that the police were raiding apartments to look for folks whose visas were expired so we stayed indoors and waited. Junior banged on the door intently and we wondered what was happening. He was speaking in a slurred voice and sounded like he was staggering around the place. Another friend in the apartment shouted to me that I should not open the door since it could be a trap but out of compassion and grace for Junior, I could not leave him hanging on his own.

Once the door was opened, eight to ten police officers ran through the door and arrested all of us on the spot. They booked me and I was sentenced to prison for three months from having an expired visa, which is a huge offense in a country like India. Now I had plenty of time to think and reflect on my life because now I was spending three months in confinement with no friends, no family, and no one to talk to. While in prison, I thought about what I would do when I came back out and if I would be deported.

I saw many things with these eyes of mine, from jail suicides and killings to fights and stabbings. We were discriminated against as black people in the prisons of India. Whenever there was a riot between a random Nigerian and an Indian prison group, the officers of the prison would randomly beat the Nigerian inmates on their knees. We were always on heightened alert because it was not uncommon to be beaten at any given time for unknown random things. It was hard to rationalize how some of us were put into a prison with hardcore criminals whilst we were just guilty of having an expired visa. Tears fell from my eyes from sunup to sundown, fearful that I would not survive this torturous confinement much longer. The food was awful, and the heat was unbearable since there was no air conditioning.

At the point of me leaving the prison at the end of my time

served, before I could sign out and collect my belongings, it was already 12:30 in the morning, when an Oga [powerful person] named Chukwudi came to greet me and take me home. Upon meeting him, we greeted each other but I quickly learned from experience, not to inquire about what others did for a living. Not knowing was better than knowing. Mr. Chukwudi, who was also from Imo state, became the mediator to my family and my lawyer while I was in prison. He asked me to come to his home and offered me a place to stay. As we drove away from the prison, that became a distant memory in the window frame, we pulled up to another Nigerian restaurant. It was my first meal outside of the prison walls and a time to savor what good cooking felt like again. Word got around the Nigerian community that I was released and so all sorts of folks came to visit and donated money to my upkeep. That was one thing I admired about my Igbo community. They are a people who will pull together and help each other out regardless of the situation. The next day Mr. Chukwudi asked me to have a stiff drink with him before he delivered the unexpected bad news. My body tensed up as he relayed the news to me that both of my mother's twin brothers had died and were subsequently buried on that same day. I collapsed upon hearing the news. Later that day, food was made for me, but I refused one bite and instead drank myself to stupor. Passed out on the floor, Mr. Chukwudi drenched my face in water to bring me back to life. He took my phone, and I went fast asleep. I woke up the next morning and did not have an appetite to eat because I was still in shock from the three deaths in my family. I was so heartbroken because I adored my uncles and especially loved my grandmother who raised me. My drinking was my way to manage my emotions which was an emotional rollercoaster. I called UD [brother] and asked him what had happened. My family would not tell me, but little did they know, I already knew. They refused to confirm what I had already suspected and just kept telling me they wanted to make sure I was in good spirits.

Mr. Chukwudi encouraged me to be strong as he began to tell me more about my grandmother's death. As I thought about my woes in India, I also thought about how an entire generation of my family were wiped out without me saying my last goodbyes. I bawled my eyes out and wondered what my future would look like. As I continued to drink myself to stupor, I knew I could not return to the old stumping grounds that once sent me down an abyss to no tomorrow. My lawyer, who I already paid large sums of money, began the process of trying to get me processed to return to Nigeria without incident. I began my realization that I would eventually leave India and return home.

7
INVESTING IN LOVE: HEARTBROKEN WITH SORROW

*E*ach time I received a call from Naija [Nigeria], I would dread answering the phone because I felt deep inside that my family members were concerned about my wellbeing. They had already inquired countless times as to when I would get married and settle down or even return to Nigeria. I was well in my thirties, and I had neither been married nor even had one child to my name. Not having my immigration documents in order wasn't the only reason I didn't want to return to Nigeria but the fear of not meeting the expectations of my family made the shame of returning to my village too unbearable.

Remember, I once told you that in Igbo tradition, having the most successes in life brings contentment to families and amassing land, houses and a marriage is what defines an Igbo man as complete in the eyes of our tradition. This very stringent expectation kept me away from my village and out of Nigeria for nearly a decade or so. I hated feeling unaccomplished and so I told myself I would start scrambling to find a damsel I could call my own. Back then I never believed in love but for me that wasn't enough motivation to ignore pursuing a woman's touch.

After all, I was the man in charge, and she would fall into her role as my future wife and the mother of my unborn children. Right?

One day as I was walking through an African grocery store, I bumped into a beautiful woman who was picking some tomatoes in the market. Her name was Chinwe and as I listened to her talk with the store clerk, I could tell by her accent that she was a Nigerian woman. When I approached her to ask where she was from, she told me that she came from a mixed family. I tried to get her number, but she refused to give it to me. Each time I would check in at the store to track her down, she would say she was not interested. After many rejections, I canvassed the area I knew she frequented and asked the neighbors where she was living. One day while riding around the neighborhood, I spotted her and struck up another conversation. This time was different because she offered to exchange numbers with me. Our conversations on the phone were lengthy and a lot of fun because she was such a great listener. Chinwe was always respectful and had everything I was looking for in a Nigerian woman. This led to our relationship blossoming into something beautiful and special. She moved into my apartment, and we began to live together like a couple. I was so into Chinwe that I invested my own money into opening a restaurant for her to find financial stability because I saw a future with her, as husband and wife.

As time passed, her true colors began to show, and I realized there would be trouble in paradise. For starters, she refused to do her own laundry, she disliked cooking, was not into doing house chores and did not particularly like assuming the role of a wife in the future I envisioned for us. Though her behavior disappointed me greatly, I was extremely patient with Chinwe and gave her time to mature into a better woman. It was my wish that she would be more versatile and nurturing towards me. As the surface peeled back, the little things became obvious, like her tendency to lie. She had told me that she was a graduate from a university and several months later, her friends had informed me that she had dropped out. When there are lies, there can be no trust in my book. How can I make a home with someone who I am unable to trust and, even worse, had no home training? To each is its own but if I come home from a long day at work and you are home all day, it's not the nicest feeling to come home to a house with no food that is chaotic with things scattered everywhere…a home I must come back to and clean up myself after being tired and exhausted. There was only so much I could take before we had a come to Jesus moment.

With time, she became more complacent, not just in our home but in our business partnership. It even got so out of control that her time and attention extended to flirting with one of our customers. This young man became a frequent fixture around our restaurant and, eventually was a frequent fixture in her bedroom. Not only did our relationship become frustrating, but it was also very stressful. I began to spend more time outside of the home meditating on what steps I should take next. I was just trying to do the right thing and be the man my family back home envisioned for me. I wanted to be that proud Igbo son, Igbo brother, Igbo uncle, Igbo husband and father with a wife, his own properties, and successes. But why was it all falling apart when I had invested so much in this woman?

Ultimately, we sat down and talked through our problems and had a mutual understanding of our departure from the relationship. Call me weak, call me a simp but as a man I was okay with this woman getting something from me because I loved her, and I wanted her to be happy and comfortable. With that, I left her and her new boyfriend the restaurant and moved out of town and on with my life, never to see them again. Even to this day, friends back there have informed me that they are still operating the restaurant in India. I no longer hold grudges and, fact, I am happy for them because I have been placed on a different path with a different person who was made just for me and me for her.

* * *

It's true that her actions led to me being heartbroken since I invested my time and money into her, and she ran off with another man but that wasn't the end of my journey. It devastated me tremendously and made it hard to be vulnerable to women since I already had trust issues, but I have learned to love again and so can you.

8
HOW HITTING ROCK BOTTOM TRANSFORMED MY SPIRITUAL LIFE

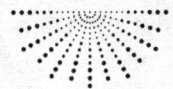

By this time, I had moved to a new city to start my life all over again. I had lost my woman, and I was looking for a new lease on life. I reconnected with a Nigerian community of men outside of the major cities and even began to mingle within the Pakistani Muslim community. They were very helpful in my time of need and often supplied basic items I needed to survive. While living in this new town, I relied on a passion only my family knew about and that was my culinary skills. In Nigeria, before coming to India, I had desires of moving to Canada, and so I had enrolled in a Culinary Arts school and completed a certification as a culinary chef.

Not many people know this about me, but I am a trained chef who enjoys cooking Nigerian and African delicacies and cuisines. I am a creative person who strives to experiment in the kitchen and create new things out of old traditions. The little money I was able to save from my restaurant business with my ex-girlfriend Chinwe was enough for me to relocate to a small town in India and began the side hustle of cooking out of my apartment.

I would cook several Nigerian pastries and fried dishes and

PURPOSE FROM ADVERSITY

deliver it to several local restaurants and grocers. Many establishments would buy it, and this generated income for me to survive and take care of my living expenses. I continued to stay in touch with my relatives back home but would only call when I needed to. The less I could say, the better for me since I was especially haunted by their demands for me to return to Nigeria.

My fear of being perceived as a nobody made me stubborn to the truth of returning home even when I lived "hand to mouth" trying to stay afloat in a new unfamiliar place. Eventually I raised enough money to get back into the business of selling cotton T-shirts and hair products to people in India locally as well as back home in Nigeria.

This retail exportation business boomed at a rate where I could buy more land in Nigeria and raise money to have some financial stability while I thought of what my next move was. One evening I went onto Facebook and met a woman named Tina. She was an African American woman from Pennsylvania who was also a single parent. She was one of the most beautiful women I have ever laid my eyes on. Such a stunning body and face that any man would want to get her time and attention.

Our time differences were hours apart and so we had to make time to talk with each other while balancing our schedules. She was not working and was a full-time stay-at-home mother while I did my business to get by. We talked for hours when time would permit, and video chatted almost every day. As time passed, I noticed that Tina enjoyed doing drugs, smoking weed, and drinking way too much alcohol. Every time she would call me, she was indulging herself in one or a combination of all three. Tina's appeal quickly dwindled right before my eyes as by now she had lacked the allure of exuding the wife material energy that I was seeking in a life partner. People may say that I am judgmental but, in my eyes, as I observe women, I always look to see who has what it takes to be a good mother to my unborn kids. That is the Igbo tradition and upbringing in me. If they are engaging in things that would make them unfit mothers, that usually makes me very uninterested in pursuing them for long term relationships.

I also did not like her behavior because she would curse her son out and talk to him in a very demeaning and uncaring manner. This extended to me when she would get upset with me. I often wished she was more respectful and valued herself more to show self-love and decency. I envisioned my life in America with Tina and thought about how often she might call the police on me if she got upset or kick me out of the house if I angered her and that made me consider her just as a friend and nothing more.

Tina eventually told me that she would not want to be with me anymore because she was afraid I was going to use her for an American permanent residency card [green card]. This saddened me because I am an honest man who speaks his mind freely and, though being in America does provide opportunities, it isn't enough for me to act desperate and let someone abuse or disrespect me just in the name of moving there. I still want to be respected as a man and given the chance to be the head of the household like my tradition dictates. I respect women so much, but I also know what gender roles should look like in a home and the expectation that follows that structure, so things are running organically. I am a giver and a lover, and I will do any and everything for the woman that I love but with that said, I still need to feel like a respected man in my own home.

Feeling alone and down with the way everything was turning out in my life, I began to reminisce about what if I had finished university in Nigeria instead of leaving a few years short of graduating. I started thinking about what if I had made better choices for my life instead of looking to make quick money. I spiraled into a state of depression and began to drink myself into a stupor. Each time I came home, I began to drink one bottle after the next, hoping to blank out the memories of failures in life and disappointments.

Then one day while browsing online, I came across another website that was a social media site for meeting adults. Here I sent a message to a woman name Sylvia, and she responded back. My mind was open and ready to date women from other regions because I was still very much heartbroken over the way Chinwe had treated me. Sylvia was a very sweet soul but was a woman who was severely physically disabled. She was acquiring a doctorate degree, was financially stable and was well on her way to an esteemed career in academia when she had a stroke that left her physically disabled. She too was an African American woman but from the southern region of the United States in a town somewhere in Tennessee.

In such a state of depression over her own misfortunes, Sylvia would often think of contemplating suicide and so I took it upon myself to pray with her and be her friend who she could rely on. Each day we would meet in the evenings and I would pray with her, and this helped me to develop a stronger relationship with my Creator. Our relationship blossomed so fast that her parents and brother quickly saw me as a familiar face within the family.

We grew so strong together and bonded over many things and whenever she was feeling gloomy, I was her listening ear and support system. I would always try to make her feel loved and wanted. My emotional support helped her to become more comfortable with talking to others and valuing herself more. She came to love me dearly and appreciate my presence in her life. Through her, I joined several groups that promoted cancer awareness and stroke victim recovery. I vowed that one day when I visited the United States, I would visit her and continue to give her my friendly support even if I was married to someone else.

During this time, my faith became stronger in my Creator,

and I began to fast and pray about my situation. I wanted movement in the right direction and a breakthrough to find my purpose in life and so I opened my heart to receiving peace and comfort in my meditative sessions. I avoided things of the physical realm like fornicating and turned to a life of celibacy. I began to take care of my mental health and emotional well-being and gave myself the time to try to find out who I was. I prayed day and night and looked within myself for a higher calling upon my life so I could hopefully find my true potential.

During this time, I also followed and listened intently to the words of my most esteemed mentor, Mr. Steve Harvey. He has done so much for my life in more ways than he will ever realize. Through him I have learned to trust the process, have an open heart, and mind and grow through my mistakes. His mentorship has helped me to love women better and listen to my inner voice to find balance in pursuit of improved mental health and self-care.

9
IMMIGRATION BARRIERS: SURVIVING MY FEARS AND STRUGGLES

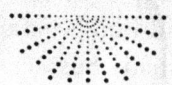

Although I was doing business and traveling around India, I finally admitted to myself and came to grips with the fact that I had an expired visa. I had returned to the country on a training visa which at the time was not allowed to be extended. This made it very difficult for me to buy property, go to school, live freely, or find a stable job outside of hustling. This was when I decided to get an immigration lawyer named Veronica. She wanted me to pay an upfront amount of 2000 dollars to get the case dropped but for me it was an overpriced amount with no real benefits. I later realized through the court system I didn't need to pay that amount of money, which meant my lawyer had taken me for a ride. That's the price you pay for being a foreigner in an unfamiliar place where people seek out opportunities to take advantage of you if you are new to a system.

Why did I have to go through all of this when all I had was an expired visa? From being beaten up in a prison and treated unfairly to being thrown in a jail cell with criminals who did worst crimes than my own. Sleeping near the likes of murderers and rapists while all I did was overstay a one-year visa was tormenting. Life in this place was not easy. There would be immigration raids to search and frisk foreigners to verify if they had legal documentation. From trying to escape that to being discriminated against, it was difficult to navigate this landscape without walking on eggshells.

There were times when police officers would bust down my door and come in to search my home for any illegal activities such as scamming and drug dealing. Most times these actions were preceded by fake reports from neighbors who claimed they saw Africans around doing nefarious things. Luckily, my hands were clean from shady business deals and so I would be given the promise of surviving another day. This was all possible thanks to an immigration document that my lawyer had given me to allow me to legally stay in India while I was being processed for being out of status. Each month like clockwork, I checked in with immigration, the way a hardened criminal checks in with their probation officer. Immigration was tracking my every movement to ensure I was staying out of trouble and physically present within India.

Even with this legal document, I kept a low profile because I was not safe and didn't feel safe in a place where people were anti-immigrant and anti-African. I avoided places where they would be asking for verification documents, and I was limited in my opportunity explorations. I ensured that I avoided any arguments or incidents that could lead to a fight because any and everything could quickly escalate into catching a case or going to jail. Being a black man in India leaves you with a target on your back and that is not an overstatement. For some, this isn't a reality but for others like me, that has been our experience. One I have lived and one I am reminded of each time I see clips of dead African bodies that come up each day on the news.

One evening around 6 o'clock, I was taking a ride in a taxi and the driver initially charged me 200 rupees but once I got to my destination, upon seeing where he was dropping me off, he increased the fare to 300 rupees. I told him that this was not the agreement that we had and asked him to give me back my correct change. As I reached to take some of my money back, he began to shout that I was a thief and everyone in the vicinity, without knowing what was really happening, began to kick, attack, and throw stones at me. There was blood spilling from my ears, lips, and face from the crashing of fists and objects all over my body. I barely pulled my aching body up and dashed toward a nearby house where I was prevented from entering. Instead, I was pushed back into the arms of my attackers, who continued to beat me. By this time, I had already passed out when a good Samaritan Indian man came to my aid, woke me up and had told me everything would be ok. He shouted at my attackers who were young Indian men and threatened to call the police on them. The young men turned their anger towards the Samaritan but eventually ran off when he began to call the police.

I was so terrified because even with my injuries, I had no residency papers. I was afraid of what would happen to me if immigration thought I was up to trouble although it was through no fault of my own. All I was guilty of was being in the wrong place, speaking up for fairness and decency while in the wrong skin. The good Samaritan put me in a taxi and sent me on my way to my home. From that day, I was on edge wherever I went, and I no longer felt safe in India. It had now become a place that could easily lead to my death because people acted first and never asked questions or used just rash means to sort out problems, especially if you were not of their kin.

Several weeks later, I was on my way to meet a friend and started out on foot near the metro station where I saw a lady who was looking at me. Her eyes were on me and I could not resist her beauty. I approached and greeted her, and she asked me where I was from. I told her I was from Nigeria. She introduced herself and inquired where I was living. At that point, her boyfriend came out of nowhere and landed a slap on my face. As I stood up to defend myself and was spotted by four Indian men who were passersby, a hail of punches came from every direction sending my head into a tailspin. How could a woman so beautiful bring such poison and pain, how could the singular act of greeting another human being almost cost someone their life? Her boyfriend, who by this time was enraged that I had spoken to his woman, landed a thunderous blow to the back of my head with his helmet sending me unconscious to the ground. As I fell to my feet and was bleeding all over the ground, I was holding onto hope that someone would save me, but the men scattered. Luckily the metro police transported me to the hospital, and I recuperated where I was treated. Never again could I look at an Indian woman the same way; even if she were to greet me with a friendly smile, I would still feel unsafe and in a state of heightened danger.

Some very simple indifferences that could be easily resolved, misunderstandings sadly escalate to grave situations that could cost any African man his life. Even when in jail, when the United Nations workers would ask us if we were mistreated or starved, we dare not admit to that or we would be beaten to a pulp by the Indian correction officers on the orders of the prison administration. They would even keep the deposits of African expatriates; and if you inquired about your rights to it, they would threaten to call the immigration officials on you so you could be arrested or deported.

Africans in India are living in fear unless they are one of those fearless scammers or drug peddlers who have amassed wealth and have security to protect themselves from a system that doesn't like their kind there. If they advertise an apartment for 10,000 rupees and you are not an Indian, especially an African, they will quote you at double the rate of 20,000 rupees. If you are driving a motorcycle out on the road as an African, they automatically assume that you are drug peddling. They will call the cops on you and sometimes even follow you to your destination to verify who you are. Why is the system this way? We are all humans who deserve to be treated fairly with decency and respect. We need more human compassion and humane interactions; meaningful connections that are built on memories that last and connections where we see ourselves in each other. It is better for me to live a free life than to own everything in the world and never be at rest with my soul.

10
A CHANCE ENCOUNTER LEADS TO A FOREVER PARTNERSHIP IN LOVE

Browsing online became my favorite pastime and it helped me to relax and pass the time indoors, away from the ills of the outside world. I had recently joined the Facebook page of a female Influencer from Nigeria who was going around claiming to be psychic. I really didn't believe a word about what she was saying. While in my chatting rant and banter, I started arguing online and while attempting to discredit the influencer as being phony, met a fellow chatter named Alyssa. Coincidentally, Alyssa who was from Canada, was also doing the same thing on the content creator's page. Through that, we bonded and formed a friendship.

We spoke to each other back and forth and our friendship blossomed into a close relationship. Alyssa told me stories of her past relationships, many of which seem disingenuous with stories filled with tragic endings. I also confided in her, letting Alyssa know that I too had been through some traumatic things, and we ended up being each other's support systems. One day, Alyssa told me that she wanted to introduce me to one of her friends from Canada, who happened to be white but to my dismay, she was reluctant to pursue getting to know me as she didn't trust African men. Although feeling disappointed by the prejudice perception, I let it go and asked her to keep me in mind if she had any other single friends. I was just seeking to have someone I could talk to and bond with because inside I felt loneliness. Here I was with an open heart and ready to see where destiny would take me.

Then one day Alyssa reached out to me and let me know that she had a friend named Nandi, who was a single parent and whom she had known since she was 18 years old. She had a Caribbean background but was American. She gave me Nandi's number and I called her. When I first started talking to Nandi, she told me that she was bored, and that Alyssa had told her that I was someone she could talk to as a friend. She told me that it had been some time since she had been with anyone seriously, and she wasn't looking for a relationship but just a friendship.

Our conversations went from introductions to having deep thought-provoking discussions about life, love, past experiences, and the future. I found that she was very similar to me in terms of future goals, and I felt a sense of comfort being in her company. Nandi was a little quirky in her ways and was so deeply engrossed in the concept of astrology, which made me chuckle. She kept saying that as an Aries man and Leo female, our energies were very aligned. Not a believer of such things, nevertheless, I had an open mind to what she was saying because I found her to be a bit fascinating. Nandi's personality and heart quickly reminded me of my own mother, which is one thing that drew my attention to her in a more intense way. I could feel deep within my soul that she was my twin flame and life partner even from the beginning of our phone calls. It was so early on, but I just felt those feelings so deeply it was like we had already known each other for years.

Within three months of talking, we both felt like we had

reached a point where we both knew we would be together in marriage. I was one year older, and she and I both had been through many traumatic hardships that were similar in nature, but, more importantly, we both knew what we wanted out of life, and it aligned. Around this time, my exit papers to leave India had been processed and it was time for me to depart India and meet Nandi in Nigeria. After all the problems, suffering and hardships in India, I was finally meeting someone who had grown to love me just the way I was. Someone who loved me beyond the money in my pockets and the lack of formal education in my head. Is this not what many pray for? I kept thanking the Lord that he had connected me through a mutual friend with a woman who appreciated me and loved me dearly and who I adored with my life.

A woman who cared about my heart and my emotions and not material things. Nandi was a woman with kids of her own, but it didn't matter to me because she had so much going for her. She was an educated woman with a glaringly bright future. Thinking back to a time in India when I was approached by a prophet who informed me that I am wasting my time looking for a spouse in India because my ordained wife was overseas waiting for me. That my future wife was not going to be Nigerian because that was the will of the Gods, and sure enough it seemed like this person was Nandi. She was the one waiting on me and I was the one who would travel from a far place to be her ordained life partner.

I began to make plans to introduce Nandi to my entire family and my village kinsmen because I knew right then and there that she was my future wife. I boarded my flight from India traveled through Kenya, then landed in Nigeria and then from Abuja to Imo State. It was a long time coming, a decade gone, the prodigal son was returning. Disembarking the plane, I almost kissed the ground, for I was back home, a mendicant in

India but a King in my own country, Mama Africa, here I am. Meanwhile, Nandi had flown to Washington DC, gone through several processes to get a Nigerian visa before returning to Texas where she lived. Fearful of heights, she was terrified to get on that plane but only love was leading the way. She booked her flight to Abuja from Dallas Fort Worth Airport to fly in to see my family and meet me. I was ecstatic and could hardly contain myself at the realization that I would be meeting the woman who made my heart quiver and my body do those funny butterflies in the tummy thing that all the adult romance novels bragged about.

My parents cried when they first made eye contact with me. They had not seen me for several years and people from the village from near and far came to greet me. They all wanted to know how I was doing and celebrated with me for one entire week to welcome me back. I had the opportunity to pray, eat and dance with my village people. They made me feel at home like I should. I wanted to be with the love of my life and so the traditional marriage preparations were underway. A full entrée of Igbo wedding artifacts, from wrappers to jewelry, payment for venues, his and her measurements, invitations, and food supplies all booked and ready only to be met with grave disappointment. My beloved future wife, Nandi called me to tell me that she would not be coming. She informed me that the US consulate had warned her that things were unstable in Nigeria due to the elections, and she was advised to stay in the United States. I had the biggest shock of my life and so did my family. My shock turned to anger as I reflected on the money that was invested in this planned affair, that was supposed to be one we would hold as memorable, our traditional wedding day.

We both made so many arrangements and I knew she was fully prepared to come here because she had bought so many wonderful gifts for my family and her ticket had been purchased. My fury wouldn't let me rest and I became a lion. Everyone around me could see a difference in my attitude. After thinking of all the troubles I'd had in India, this was supposed to be my beautiful ending, but it seemed to be so out of reach, so far yet so near.

What was I going to do right now? How could I get to marry the love of my life? I packed my things and went back to the village to be with my parents. I stayed here all through the first three months of being back in Nigeria. This same woman I loved so much had a beautiful heart made of gold. She stood by me and let me know that even if she couldn't come to Nigeria, she would still one day marry me. A person often meets his destiny on the road he took to avoid it and so I became patient and trusted the process just as I did when I was in India. For the past two years of our courtship, she has been my backbone throughout all my problems and issues. She is someone who makes me very happy, and I plan to have her as my forever life partner.

On thing I love about this woman is that she is very resourceful and proactive. Even though she was not physically with me, she still encouraged me to build a career for myself. Despite being frustrated with her not coming, she kept pushing me to get my ducks in a row and to work on developing myself. I kept wondering what I could possibly do with my life at the age of thirty- eight years old. She told me that I was never too old to learn or grow and that I had to be more intentional about my plans toward life so I could be comfortable in my old age. My family was completely disappointed and irritated because they did not understand that timing was important. It was not the right time for us to marry but only God knew that. I had to calm them down and tell them to leave the situation alone. My baby told me that I needed to take the bull by the horns and create my own life canvas. She said you must have something of your own because you have a purpose in this life, and you are not reaching your potential. January came around and she again told me told me to choose a career for myself. I sat down and meditated about it. I then told her that I would like to do welding because it reminds me so much of what civil engineering entailed, which was my major in college. It was also something I could complete in a shorter space to time to transition into the job market since I felt like time was not on my side.

Nandi called me up one day and told me that she would support me in my efforts and registered me with an online welding course through an American University. Though I was elated at the prospect of improving my career and life, I was intimidated because getting back into the motions of schooling made me feel overwhelmed. It had been so long since I had to study or learn in a university setting that I sort of felt like I missed my way. She reminded me that she had paid a hefty amount for that course and that I needed to get it completed by fire or force. See Nandi has a teaching background, education is so important to her, and I think that is where her encouragement comes from. She means well and wants to see me be successful and winning in the realm of life. This is one of the reasons that I adore her. She is a builder and a creator, and it comes quite naturally to her to plan and execute tasks effectively. At this point Nandi gave me an ultimatum, she let me know that if I decided not to complete the welding program, she would break off the relationship because she needed to know that I was a serious man who could bring something to the table. My baby blocked me and changed her number. I wept for several days because now I had let my fear of compromising my chance at keeping love in my life. I begged Alyssa to beg Nandi to reconsider because I had made up my mind to complete the course. After all it was for my own development, but why was I so scared? I called her on an unknown number, and she hung up on me. Then I called her on another number and asked her to please hear me out before she decided not to talk to me again. This time I told her that she needed to be patient with me and let me get through this thing slowly. Several weeks into the course and I was starting to feel like I had enough. Knowing Nandi, she was checking into the course to ensure that I was completing my work and passing. The phone rang and she was at the end of the line complaining that I was not getting any work done. Next thing I knew, she had called all my brothers and told them what I was not doing. So now I had three angry individuals berating my lack of action and letting me know that I was not doing enough. I began to pray again to ask my Creator to give me strength to get through this because it wasn't as easy as people thought it was. I was ready to give up, but she kept encouraging me to be responsible and get through the challenge without giving up on myself. Two weeks passed by, and I started slacking again, not being consistent with turning in my assignments. My baby blocked me again. I just couldn't understand why I was so distracted but I was trying. I was scared out of wits, and I tried to reach Nandi, but she ignored me. I turned to prayer once again, seeking favor from my Creator that if she truly was for me then she would return to me and if not, then she would permanently go away. God answered my prayers, and she unblocked me. I was ecstatic when I was able to finally complete my Welding course! This gave me an opportunity to work in the welding industry, thanks to the love of my life being near me every step of the way. She has been by my side and has taught me not to chase money but to find more meaningful things in life. She was brought into my world to teach me so many lessons that have helped to improve the quality of my life. She completes me in so many ways and I feel saddened when she is not by my side. She is the Yin to my Yang.

Reflecting on all the hardships I had experienced in India,

this love and progress feels like a final pay off. The Creator has shown mercies upon my life since I chose the longer but righteous path to follow, though tougher, free from the easier fast life, filled with illicit activities, this is my divine retribution. She is a blessing to my family, my unborn children and, most importantly, me. Our love has never been strained even when we have our ups and downs, our quarrels, my baby, and I always reconcile. Thanks to her support and encouragement, I have a career in welding, and I can work as a welder in any place in the world. I love this woman with my every fiber, and she has brought the best out of me. She is a Godsend to my life and makes me smile, laugh, and feel special.

We have many plans together for the future. I want to be the only man that puts a complete smile on her face. To just think, back in the day I was that man who would never consider marrying a woman with kids but it's funny how love works because today, that same man has fallen deeply in love with Nandi and her four children. All those superficial restrictions I once held women to went through the door because she represented everything I wanted in a woman, and I was more than happy to accept her with her lovely children from other relationships. Those children welcome and love me like I am their own father and they have shown me so much love, respect, and support. They see me as a father figure, someone they can love and seek advice from. When I think of my past life in India, I know without an atom of doubt that God has kept me alive to take care of those who need me in their lives, that is Nandi and our kids. He had a purpose for my life, and it was to meet this woman and experience all the colors of love. Her youngest child, a beautiful little girl, often refers to me as her dad and constantly inquiries when I would be marrying her mom. You can see the kind of close bond they have for me. My beautiful mother-in-law, who has been in support of our relationship and who has always helped in one way or the other, is a positive force in our union. She has brought ideas to the table to help us to become a stronger and stable family dynamic, even to the point that she has invested money into my career to help me take an English immigration exam.

Who am I and why have I received all this love from this family? My clean heart and positive energies boomeranged into the universe have reciprocated energies my way through the Charles family. If not this woman, then count me out of ever marrying in this life. I am so grateful to be a part of this family, they have been very hospitable and welcoming to me. Having family support is important in Igbo tradition. If families do not accept your spouse, it is hard to proceed with marriage.

My only regret is that I will never get to meet Nandi's elder sister who passed away from suicide before we met. My future wife talks about how important she was to the science community and how much love their parents had for her. She told me about her educational accomplishments, a PhD in Pharmacology and how much she served in scientific research regarding brain tumors and patent law.

My future wife and I pray together at night that we should find our purpose in life and for the Creator to show us the way, bless us, and forgive our sins. I am the happiest man alive because I never thought I'd find my soul mate or a purpose for living; but I have now. The relationship I have with Nandi is one where I plan to marry her for a lifetime. I have accepted her with her children because of the beauty that is within her heart and the beauty that radiates from within her soul.

When I first met Nandi, I remember telling her how much I loved Steve Harvey. With the eye roll and chuckle, she said, "That's nice", and proceeded to lend a listening ear as I rambled on about what I learned from his teachings. Most of the teachings I have embraced came from watching his television show. On a consistent basis, Steve has said that love can come from out of the blue and once you find it, it is a major life changing event. He has played a big role in my love life. He is the reason I was able to accept Nandi in her ways and love her and her kids. These four children have different fathers but still I could not let this woman go because what I see in her is love, sincerity, peacefulness, and patience. She has been down a long road and kissed many frogs along the way, but she is resilient, and she is exactly what I need to find peace and love. When I hear her story, I realize that her situation is a unique one. I am looking forward to putting that ring on her finger and marrying her outside of a courthouse. I want our marriage to be in a church in a big wedding venue before all our family members, friends, and acquaintances. I am proud of her and want the entire world to know that.

I can say at this stage in my life I feel more complete, and I am able to accomplish many things. I see myself as an upcoming billionaire in energy, so my hope is that it materializes itself in the physical realm. My partner is such a great asset in my journey of life. This is the only time in my life that I have felt settled and at home. I told my future wife that I wanted to adopt her kids and have them as my own to show her how important they are to me. To show her how much I love and appreciate them. I also told my future wife that I want to have a child or two with her biologically. I want to bond with my future wife in every way and for me as an Igbo man, this is part of our traditional structure. The birth of children is very important in Igboland, especially our male children because they are the ones who carry on our names, our legacies, and our lineages. My own parents have celebrated 54 years of marriage and Nandi's parents have celebrated 45 years of marriage and I believe that our marriage will also last the test of time because we are very compatible, and we both come from lineages that have respected and worked through their marital journeys.

I am a fully committed Igbo man, and as such, I told my future wife that if I ever come to live in the United States and I were to join my ancestors, it would be my desire to have my body be transported back to Nigeria for proper Igbo burial rites. I would also like Nandi to return to Nigeria with me one day and settle down there when she is in her old age because I want my future wife to be buried beside me in keeping with the tradition of my village.

11
A RETURN TO UMUELEAGWA AND FINDING MY TRUE PURPOSE IN LIFE

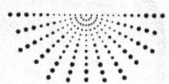

I have very strong interests in my Igbo traditions and values. When I came back to my village town, my parents were now retired, I got to see firsthand accounts of my dad suffering from dementia. It was a very sad thing for me to witness because he was always a strong and fierce military man. It was hard to see him in a situation where he was vulnerable. One day my dad was lost, wandered around for nearly two weeks, and some folks kidnapped him and held him for a ransom.

A young woman who was passing through town saw my dad lying in the street injured with bruises. She showed concern and compassion and took him to a police station where he received medical treatment. Thankfully someone recognized him and reported it to the people in our village where we were able to reconnect with him and bring him back home safely. It was one of the things you realize is part of the aging process and yet we have to be respectful of our parents because they once took care of us and now we have to take care of them.

Being in the village and living with my parents, it has been a blessing in disguise. We are surrounded by organic foods grown fresh from the farm; a scene wrapped in nature with loud thumping sounds of Naija [Nigerian] cultural masquerade tunes pulsating through unpaved dirt roads. All cultural traditions I missed but embrace. Since living here, I have had the opportunity to visit celebrations, burials, and ceremonies as well as meetings to engage in projects that uplift my Imo community. No matter how much of a success I become in life, I can never forget my culture and village because it is so deeply ingrained in me that I cannot depart from it. This village is comprised of people with integrity and a place where immorality is not welcomed. We are law-abiding citizens and we do not have a strong presence of criminal activity. We are a united people who work tirelessly to uplift our own. After all, it was a place, where during the Biafra war, the antelopes were instrumental in saving the people of Umueleagwa. Antelopes are known for eating pumpkin leaves and pumpkin seeds. During the war, when the Biafra crops were destroyed and my people were not able to eat anything, we saw the antelopes feasting on the pumpkin leaves and seeds. Using the antelopes as a guide, our people followed suit and used the same plants to find food during a time when thousands were facing famine and starvation, which led to large numbers of deaths. The foods that the antelopes identified for us saved the lives of many Igbo people in my village.

In our appreciation of these animals, we have renamed our city after them and around every five years, we celebrate the antelopes because of the contributions they made to our survival as a people. We now use the pumpkin seeds as a representation of our kola nut [symbolic Nigerian nut]. In 2022 when I touched down in my village, coincidentally, the antelope festival was also being celebrated. It was a grand time of merriment where many major attractions were on display by the natives of my land. No one in our community is allowed to eat antelopes for any reason. Other neighboring villages that hunt these animals are not allowed to exercise that in our village. In fact, there have been times when hunters from other places have inadvertently run the antelopes into our village which then become a safe space against meeting their deaths. I think they know we are guardians to them because each time we hold festivals in their memory, many of them can be seen parading around to the festivities.

Another interesting fact about our village is people from Umueleagwa are forbidden from marrying another person from the same village. Instead, we must marry someone from outside of our village. The logic behind this is that one person is connected to every person in the village and so to avoid marrying your own relatives, people in my village must marry an outsider to multiply. Most of the people here are Catholic and are very friendly and hospitable towards foreigners, helping each other move up political and financial ladders. We stand on the principle of being our brother's keepers.

If siblings fight each other, it is considered an abomination whereby fines typically ensue. Those Umueleagwa people from the diaspora are also very connected to my village. Most of them are within Igbo association organizations that unite them and every year they will pool their finances and support or sponsor a development project for infrastructure back in the village. We are a people of builders, shakers, and movers. We are very much an enterprising group of people who strive to build and develop our community and our people.

While in the village, I was able to start up a chicken farm of about 170 chickens. I cultivated a vegetable garden and learned several farming techniques. I was exposed to planning, building with my hands, growing things on my own and developing a good time management system. I also participated fully in the funeral of our late King, Noble Okeahialam and took part in his burial ceremony.

I would travel between my village and Owerri to take part in my welding internship. Here I was able to acquire many unique skills and techniques in welding. It has enabled me to create doors, weld sheets together, fasten pipes and read construction blueprints. I made huge gains in this career field, and I am very confident that I will have a future career as a welder when I leave Nigeria. I am also now able to create my own design and product prototypes with my bare hands that I can price and sell to customers as a mobile welder. My newly acquired skills in welding has opened many doors for me and has strengthened my ability to seek financial stability.

Being in my village at this point has helped me to appreciate life more because I see people who have been struggling and suffering, and so I have learned to be thankful for what I have. There are orphans here, people who are getting by with very little, people who are worse off than me, helping me to realize that I am blessed with a sense of direction and belonging. It has taught me to have grace for myself. When I think of what I have passed through and where I am now, I realize that I have a purpose in life.

Despite the things they are going through and how ineffective the Nigerian government has been, I make it my duty to gather and encourage the younger people to learn a skill or trade. I see people selling land just to go abroad only to end up in worse situations than I was. I let them know that they need something better to fall on in life before making leaps overseas. I encourage them to not be desperate or they may end up in situations that are traumatic with hardships.

I have learned more about myself as a man and as a person in general. My interactions with people are very meaningful and I have learned to work with people, young and old, from all facets of my community. Being back here has reintroduced me to my culture and tradition and it has made me fall in love with my culture all over again.

I have learned the values of embracing people just the way

they are in their differences, and I have really been transformed and changed from the person I once was yesterday to who I am today. The community has shown countless times that they will come together as a team to work across the aisle to create initiatives that benefit all the citizens who live here. Here I have been motivated to work harder and develop a solid work ethic to get things done. Being here challenged me to step up my game and be a better version of myself.

12

A CRITICAL ANALYSIS OF HOW FAILURES SHORTCHANGE OUR YOUTHS

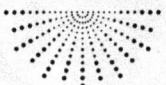

This section of my book is very close to my heart because it was one of the reasons, I initially left Nigeria with hopes of achieving a dream of pursuing wealth and status. Nigeria is a country with a robust portfolio of natural resources and wealth but with gross mismanagement of funding and resources has had serious impacts on the quality of life for our young people.

When the youths are left out of the process of building a country, people often feel marginalized. Graduates are unable to find a job when they leave university, setting the country up for a field full of undervalued, overworked, and underpaid citizens who will sometimes turn to illicit activities to get by.

We have a serious problem with capital flight in Nigeria because many professionals aren't paid a salary on a consistent basis and so when they come upon opportunities, they are migrating in mass droves. When we travel overseas to places like the United States, Canada, and United Kingdom we often see our Nigerian professionals working there because they do not feel valued in their own country. Our law enforcement, who are supposed to be upstanding public servants, are instead the kings of bribery. But even they must use such tactics to support their families as their salaries have well underpaid them. How can you give a hungry man a gun and not expect him to do bad things?

Nigeria needs to rewrite their constitution, not today but since yesterday. It was designed only to protect the politicians and the wealthy. It needs to be a document that protects all citizens. We have a system where the rich are getting richer and the poor are getting poorer. There is no such thing in Nigeria as doing things the right way. It is only in Nigeria that you will find out that there is such a thing as a ghost worker. This is a warm body who is not even living in Nigeria but is on the country's payroll. It is only in my country where people do not get things by merit, but you get appointed by nepotism and tribalism. This is the reason why the young people are fed up and frustrated with the system. The reason why they prefer to go abroad and spend their whole lives there with no interest in returning. They cannot find an ounce of peace of mind within the confines of their own homeland. Most developments in Nigeria that benefit its citizens are mostly done by outside forces in the diaspora not the appointed government.

How can you stop younger men and women from scamming in Nigeria if you have no other alternatives for them, like jobs after graduation or a program to help them better themselves? How can you ask people to quit scheming and find ways to cheat the system when all the role models they look up to are also scheming the system through bribery, extortion, and coercion? Nigeria can do so much better for its people but why are they choosing not to? Ninety percent of those internet scammers are college graduates. What does this say about the destruction the Nigerian government is doing to its youth? Imagine creating digital learning hubs for these young people and teaching them cybersecurity skills that they could use in cybersecurity jobs created right here. This could change the fate of these young graduates and keep them on the track of long-term professional growth and development which will benefit Nigeria.

Nigerian youths are instead running into desperate situations overseas in some places like Asia and Europe where many face death or murder and everyone is hush hush about it. Most of these young men are not born to do drugs and scamming but are instead dabbling into it out of desperation to survive and frustration with limited resources. My people are not asking for much; just better infrastructure and twenty-four hours of electricity running without constant blackouts. They are not asking for much, just a steady stream of income that they earned and respect for their hard work in their career fields. They are not asking for much, just a free education system from kindergarten to the 12th grade so that all educational barriers are removed for all kids prior to attending college. Interesting that none of the politicians prefer to put their money where their mouths are and enroll their own kids into schools in Nigeria. Instead, they send their own children off to schools overseas while those who they manage back home are left to school here. I guess what is good for the goose isn't good for the gander.

The only dying hope of Nigerian politicians is to pass a legislature that will favor their social and political self-interests alone. It is only in Nigeria where someone will win an election and, a few years later, that same person will become a billionaire while supposedly being paid on a civil servant salary. It is only in Nigeria that the running candidate will know well in advance that he is going to win an election, announce it and still win it. With this trend, does fair politics really exist in this country?

As a politician who governs a population of people where over 90% of them are poverty stricken, can you say this is a politician working in the good faith of the people? How can a government bring in foreign companies to do business in our country and avoid hiring local Nigerians who are qualified? How can this be ok with our politicians? Why are they allowed to hire only foreigners and leave our citizens jobless?

The legislative body just passed a bill that they plan to import and distribute SUV jeeps for official business, a move that carries an overhead cost amounting to billions of US dollars. Meanwhile, they could have gotten the same vehicles, made locally from a business called Innoson Vehicle Manufacturing, a move that snubs their own local business enterprise and says to the world that they do not have an interest to invest in their own but other countries instead. This removes money from our economy and puts it in the hands of other governments who have no genuine interest in building our country but instead strive on exploiting our natural resources. Let's examine the highways and roads in our country. Most of them are dilapidated and filled with potholes for days. Will the government ever invest in fixing those? This is part of the provisions a government is supposed to make for its citizens. How come they keep giving contracts to these Lebanese companies to fix the roads and the end products show that the infrastructure is not getting any better? Do they think that just by saying they are giving business to a foreigner equates to having a quality product? Because as far as the eyes can see, their road fixing skills are inferior and made with subpar products that keep the road continuously damaged and eroded. It is only in Nigeria that there is a sort of preferential treatment for those with wealth and status versus those who are the have nots.

It is only in Nigeria where a fraudster or a drug king pin can return to the country and then request for police escorts when this individual has had an unscrupulous background associated shady dealings and the police officers that are public servants and owe their loyalty to the citizens of Nigeria, will provide security for them. Politicians here can be caught stealing funds from the taxpayers and natural resources then be invited to join the reigning party all while being exonerated from any wrongdoings.

We must do better for our youths so that they can have a better future. A country that invests in its future is a country with a vision for a brighter tomorrow.

13
SEEKING MY DESTINY ONE PLAN AT A TIME

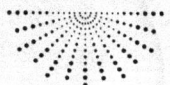

Around my late 50s and early 60s I have a desire to create an impact in Nigeria by becoming an effective politician. My passions and heart are with Nigeria, and I am a man of the people whose intentions are pure and my heart is real. I want to be able to show people that they are authentic ways of doing things. It is my duty to show people that they can trust the process and benefit from policies implemented.

I want to be able to rewrite the wrongs and help Nigerians to feel respected, valued and understood. My wish is to bring Nigerians together and to limit the tribalism. Let people be judged based on their merits and not through nepotism or status. I am a simple man with great ideas, I am a person of the people who knows exactly what they want and will work towards achieving those goals. I want to put the smile on the faces of Nigerians and to enjoy the fruits of our resources.

As a future politician, I would like to show the country that we can invest in their futures and give them the necessary training and skills to build a working class and middle-class sector in our country because as it stands, these people are the backbone of our nation. The people who work with their hands and the people who create from their minds are the ones who we need to invest in most.

As a future politician, it is important for us to build our nation around the youth and take into consideration their needs as they are the ones who will be reaping from the policies that are created. It is my desire to help lift Nigerians out of poverty so that they are cutting free from generational poverty shackles. I want to ease the capital flight risk of our qualified professionals by ensuring that they are paid better rates so that we do not lose those skilled folks who provide excellent services to our citizens. Our healthcare facilities need to be improved so that all Nigerians and even foreigners who live here can get good quality health screenings and checkups without having to take flights to the West.

I would like to be able to lift restrictions on freedom of the press, speech, and the ability to assemble in Nigeria because the media and citizen protests are an integral part in the growth of a nation. They help to inform us, inspire us, and educate us on what is relevant and pressing and what needs our immediate attention. They help to give us the necessary checks and balances so we can have better transparency and a country of leaders we can trust.

Another thing they needs to improve is our public health and epidemiological systems because we have a widespread crisis of malaria affecting most of our population. This is not only dangerous to the citizens who burden our health care systems because of it, but it is also a deterrence to foreigners who plan to visit, migrate here to do business, and make Nigeria their home. A nation that cares about the health systems is one that grows and develops people out of poverty and crises.

I think it's also necessary to investigate religious organizations that are becoming too much like a business and not operating like a non-profit that it should be. I believe that we will need to have a unit that inspects whether there is exploitation of Nigerian citizens so we can regulate these organizations and ensure that they are in alignment with consumer protections. I would like to set up a division that will closely also regulate the food industry in Nigeria and give the restaurant grades for their quality of food and sanitation. That would give restaurant owners incentives to maintain upscale standards while giving consumers the chance to make informed decisions about where they would like to eat.

Where I am from in Imo State, the development there is currently in a very inferior state in terms of infrastructure and planning. I want to bring both local and foreign investments into that city and throughout other parts of Nigeria so that people can have better quality of services and an upgraded standard of living. I want to see an expansion of the city and better security and stability in that region. It is my desire to see investments not just from the West but also from other African nations who have quality services and products we need for development.

It is also important to have fair and balanced elections conducted locally so that local politicians can have autonomy in their own local affairs which can enable local governments to create, build and empower its citizens and youths. We need to build better irrigation systems which will allow our sewage systems and waterways to flow in the right manners and prevent flooding of ponds and streams. These simple changes reduce public health crises that create microbial organisms and pathogens from spreading rapidly amongst communities. If not managed, can put a strain on our health system and increase poverty amongst those who are also living in hardships and are severely disadvantaged.

Our veterans, military families and soldiers, educators, law enforcement and public servants, need to be able to have a decent pension while in retirement. This is important because many of these individuals have given an eternity of their time to serving others and deserve to have a respectable income coming in after they have reached the age of retirement. They were the ones who educated us, protected us, instilled the law for us and filled positions that many refused to even consider.

14
STRATEGIES FOR SUCCESS AFTER FAILURES AND DISAPPOINTMENTS IN LIFE

Being on the right side of history: Let's stay away from robbing Peter to pay Paul. Do the things that are righteous and fair, following the proper script and ensuring that your business and professional decisions are from legitimate means. Ensure that your deals are done in a way that doesn't disrupt the natural order of things so that at the end of day you can have peace of mind and be in a good place spiritually and in alignment with the universe. Ensure that whatever choices you make, your future generations will be proud of you, and you do not do things to dishonor your family's name. We can control our choices but never our consequences.

Consistency: Do not throw the towel in when you meet a stumbling block in life because this is all part of growing as an adult. We must go through pillars of disappointment, obstacles, and hardships but your ability to stay on task and keep pushing towards what you want is your ability to be consistent. I did not let my problems, even when they were trying and almost broke my spirit, defeat my dreams or my aspirations in life. I continued my journey and tried different things to get to where I wanted to be. I had a growth mindset which allowed me to learn from my mistakes and build character. These things only come through showing consistency. Like a person on a weight loss journey, you don't just give up because you didn't get to your desired weight goal, you keep going and working out to attain your objectives.

Perseverance: Withstanding pressure and being patient are two traits that help us with perseverance. Good things come to those who wait can't be overstated enough because it really perfects the ability to have a plan while waiting for opportunities to come your way. When we have challenges, we must step up to the plate and tackle them head on. We must give ourselves some grace and be patient for that plan to materialize. Some people jump into things too prematurely and do not give themselves time to blossom at the right time. Do not self-sabotage yourself by prematurely taking risks that are not carefully considered or planned.

Remove Distractions: Surround yourself with positive energies that help you to grow and build yourself. If you are aware of vices or things that distract you like excessive drinking, random sex and drugs that throw you off course, remove those things from your life. Be very sure to control your emotions and do not let your emotions control you. This will go a long way in helping you to regulate your attitude and behavior around others. Always remove friends from around you that are toxic, that lead you to destructive actions or who are negative energies. You know those friends that always have something negative to say when you share good news with them. Stay clear of such friends because, ultimately, they are not interested in you growing or being happy.

Stay true to yourself: Do your best to be authentic to your identity. Try not to live up to a standard that is a mere shell of yourself. Stay connected to your inner self and the voice that leads you. Be honest with who you are and be realistic with your plans for your life. Have that heart-to-heart introspection with yourself and ensure that you are shining through in your own purpose and calling. People recognize when you are trying to be something that you are not, and so it is best to do what you were placed on this earth to achieve. The universe has a way of showing us the clues so open your eyes, accept, and embrace it.

Focus on your goals: Keep your eyes on the prize has always been a golden rule. In this part of your journey, you want to be able to keep your mind set on achieving your plans and objectives in life. When we focus on our goals, we are making plans, having target objectives, and being driven to execute things we are focused on. Whether this is a career, a project, finishing school or something that is close to your heart, it requires time and devotion.

Never give up on yourself: In the art of loving oneself, you must never give up on yourself. It is a part of self-care and self-worth. Whenever it looks like you are about to lose it all, that is usually when our headaches are coming to an end. In the race of life, once the race begins, we must keep trekking until we reach the finish line. We have no time for short cuts or breaks along the way, but rather we must stay on course and keep going. Winners never quit and quitters never win is an adage that I live by because it simply makes the case for why giving up is not an option. We must believe in ourselves because that will help motivate us to stay strong and hold ourselves to a higher calling. Even when others tell us we are a nobody and will never amount to anything, we are our own cheerleaders and support systems and there is a voice deep within that is telling us to never give up on ourselves.

ABOUT THE AUTHORS

Mr. *Eunan C. Anyaibe*

Ms. *Nandi Charles*

Mr. Anyaibe is Nigerian and was born to a family from the Igboland region of Imo State, Nigeria.

Ms. Charles was born in Guyana and is from an Afro-Caribbean background [Barbados and Guyana]. She has lived overseas for more than twenty-eight years, with twenty-three of those years spent in the United States.

* * *

Both authors are committed to a life of cultural traditions that tie in with the African diaspora experience. They enjoy collaborating to write stories that showcase cultural experiences, traditions, and value systems within the African diaspora community globally.

Thank you for purchasing our book and we hope that elements from the storyline are relatable to your own personal experiences. We also are thankful that we can use this platform to inform our readers and showcase the ideal that people can be given second chances in life to succeed and that there can be purpose acquired after adverse life events.

REFERENCES

SELECTED SOURCES FOR STATISTICAL DATA AND FACTS

UNCTAD, *Press Release Facts & Figures*, revised edition, United Nations, 2019.

Nwaubani, Adaobi, "*Remembering Nigeria's Biafra war that many prefer to forget*," BBC News, 2020.

Ighobor, Kingsley, "*Overfishing Destroying Livelihoods*," Africa Renewal, United Nations, 2017.

Boudreau, Diane, McDaniel Melissa, Sprout, Erin and Turgeon, Andrew, *Africa: Resources*, National Geographic Society, 2023.

Anyangwe, Eliza, "*10 Things Africa Has Given the World*," A Week In Africa, The Guardian Newspaper, 2015.

Blatch, Sydella, "*Great Achievements in Science and Technology in Ancient Africa*," ASBMBTODAY, 2013.

Staff Writers, "*South African Iron and Steel exports to the European Union Under Threat*," Steel Matters, 2023.

Ferris, Nick, "*How CBAM threatens Africa's sustainable development*," Carbon Markets: Energy Monitor, 2023.

U.S. National Library of Medicine, *Cesarean Section- A Brief History*, History of Medicine, 2013.

Gulley, Andrew, "*One Hundred year of cobalt production in the Democratic Republic of the Congo*," Resources Policy, 2022.

Boland, M.A and Kropschot, S. J., "*Cobalt- For Strength and Color*," USGS Mineral Resources Program, 2011.

Trento, Chin, "*What is Cobalt Used in Everyday Life*," Stanford Advanced Materials, 2023.

National Minerals Information Center, *Cobalt Statistics and Information*, USGS, 2023.

Food Empowerment Project, "*Child Labor and Slavery in the Chocolate Industry*," Food Empowerment Project, 2022.

UN Environment Program, "*Our Work in Africa*," United Nations, 2023.

Hadithi Africa, "*10 Greatest inventions that hailed from Africa*," Hadithi Africa, 2023.

Florek, Dr. Stan, "*Hand axes from Somalia and our African Origin*," Australian Museum, 2023.

Sample, Ian, "*Hand axes unearthed in Kenya are oldest advanced stone tools ever found*," Anthropology: The Guardian, 2011.

www.ingramcontent.com/pod-product-compliance
Lightning Source LLC
Chambersburg PA
CBHW070627050426
42450CB00011B/3133